POWER

to Soar

New Strength Daily
from the Father's Heart

CHARLES SLAGLE

Destiny Image Publishers
P.O. Box 310
Shippensburg, PA 17257-0310
"We Publish the Prophets"
ISBN 1-56043-101-6
For Worldwide Distribution
Printed in the U.S.A.

DEDICATION

It's pure pleasure to dedicate this pocket reminder to John and Christine Noble. Co-founders of Team Spirit, originating in Collier Row, England, this couple so radiantly reflects the heart of our Heavenly Father. These trail blazers stand out as a real dad and mom in His Kingdom.

How enriching, their friendship and input! How liberating, their courage to honor and exhibit God's reality, their fearlessness to roar with laughter at religious pomposity!

The spiritual revolution this husband and wife team is stirring in our world is awakening multitudes to *experience* the Living God.

John and Christine Noble often have been labeled as "radicals." And so they are! My wife, Paula, and I only pray that more of their refreshing radicalism will rub off on us...

ABOUT THE AUTHOR

Charles and Paula Slagle have traveled in ministry since November 1971. They've ministered in the United States, Canada, Australia, New Zealand, Singapore, Malasia and extensively in Mexico, Central America and Great Britain.

Often dubbed "prophetic psalmists," the Slagles seek to leave a legacy of new songs of triumph among God's family. They also conduct seminars with the view of helping others learn to listen to God for themselves, to experience the healing of His Father's heart.

Charles and Paula, along with their son, Bryan, live in San Antonio, Texas.

INTRODUCTION

Sometimes less is more. We don't always need all-encompassing messages. We just need timely reminders that recharge our spirits with power to soar above this mad world's unrelenting seduction.

Father God often recharges this guy through His subtle one-liners — some of which aren't so subtle! Some of His wisecracks even seem downright obnoxious! But they penetrate through my plastic, exposing my bondage to the superficial. I'm finding that the entrance of God's words truly brings light, laughter and freedom — even in those times when His words first move me to tears. But such godly sorrow always leads to healing repentance.

I'm praying these short messages will help sensitize other listeners to hear our Father's voice for themselves.

May I make one suggestion? Don't substitute this pocket reminder for reading Scripture or hearing God for yourself! Keep a small notepad and scribble down some impressions you *think* God may be imparting to you. Then stay sensitive to receive His confirmation and adjustment.

Sometimes He may confirm through Scripture — or perhaps through something written in other books or even in this one. But don't try to package Him neatly into printed pages or sources that appear overtly spiritual! Our Father speaks through circumstances, and often through unlikely people. He's even been known to speak through a donkey! So what else is new?

Just remember: Jesus endured unspeakable suffering to destroy the sin-barrier that stood between us and direct access to our Father. Nothing pleases our Lord more than our enjoying the awesome privilege of intimacy with our God that He purchased for us.

So go for it! Venture out. Just bear in mind that prayer is conversation. It involves *listening* as well as speaking.

Discover Almighty God in His Living Reality! Receive His love, and more and more you will come to love Him with all your being. Hurting hearts await the healing life that will overflow from your loving union with our Father. Only love-miracles can free a shame-shackled and cynical world...

Charles Slagle

THANK YOU

To Tish Collings, my younger sister and gifted writer, for superb editing!

To Paula, my wonderful wife, for...you name it!

To Rebecca Schroeder, for typing, typing and more typing!

To my mom, Connie Slagle; her grandchildren, Jarrod and Lindsay Collings; our son, Bryan and our secretary, Jayne Hartong, for all input.

And once again, to Cliff Hawley, for great artwork done on such generous terms!

May our Dad mightily multiply back blessing to all who have helped on this manuscript.

Are you going to let this day intimidate you?

JANUARY

Ps. 118:21-24   **1**

Cherished Child,

Are you going to let this day intimidate you? Jesus is the Everlasting Holiday I have provided for you. Rejoice, and be glad in Him!

> Yours with All Power,
> Dad

II Cor. 11:14   **2**

Innovative Child,

Beware of the spirit of antichrist. He's always offering 666 easy steps to success without Jesus!

> Love,
> Dad

Matt. 9:12; Phil. 3:12-15   **3**

Introspective Restorer,

Unless I lead you to do so, looking back hurts far more than it helps.

JANUARY

Again, child! Will you trust Me? I delight in turning blunders into blessings for the yielded and humble of heart.

Always!
Father

Matt. 13:16,17; I Cor. 2:9,10 **4**

Exhausted Child,

When will you abandon the practice of observing appearances and seek supernatural insight?

I've ordained today's challenges to nudge you toward such revelation. Adventure awaits Us. Let's enjoy!

Helpfully,
Father

I Cor. 12:4,5 **5**

Worried One,

Why should I object to doctors? I AM One!

I often enrich My children by introducing them to My friends in the medical profession.

Trust Me to lead you.

Tenderly, Faithfully,
Dad

Ps. 13:4-6   6

Child,

I love you too much to let those who victimize you live with no regrets.

Yours Faithfully,
Dad

Heb. 10:19-22   7

Exhausted Seeker,

You may enjoy My company whenever you wish. Anywhere, any night or day, any moment!

And you needn't shout across light-years of ever-expanding cosmos to reach Me.

Why reach for what you already have?

Everlastingly Yours,
Dad

Matt. 23   8

Determined Warrior,

Do you want to succeed in religion? Compete! Compare! Contrive an attractive public image and *always* maintain it. Cater to the rich, to the powerful. Never be seen with "losers." Crave human applause. Demand respect! If need be, slander and trample others to get it.

And, at all costs, avoid Reality. I remain,

Your Implacable Opponent,
Father God

Ps. 51:17 **9**

Smiling Liberator,

I enjoy your company more than you know. Not many of My children keep Me laughing the way you do.

I just want to remind you that I AM here if you ever need a shoulder to cry on.

I Love You.
Dad

Gal. 3:21-25 **10**

Determined Law Enforcer,

How will people who are fearing punishment and scrambling to survive ever find time to recognize love, let alone receive or transmit it? Threats and judgment spawn paranoia.

Paranoia breeds hate and intolerance, not holiness! Whose kingdom are you promoting?

Committed to Good News, Always!
Father

Matt. 7:12 **11**

Child,

Request granted! I AM giving you wisdom. Behave toward others as you would have them behave toward you. Expect miracles!

Trusting You Always,
Dad

Matt. 5:14-16 **12**

Concerned Disciple,

What is the "local church"? It is My royal children loving their neighbors.

Helpfully,
Father

I Cor. 13:4 | 13

Wounded One,

You gave up for a moment, but I didn't. Nothing has changed between Us. Will you believe Me?

Forever Supporting You,
Father

Phil. 4:4-7 | 14

Weary Child,

Keep rejoicing, and allow everyone to see My gentle mercy in you. I AM near. Refuse to worry! Express your every need to Me with thankfulness, cherished one.

Peace that transcends earthly reason is yours for the receiving.

Dad

Eph. 6:7,8 | 15

Frustrated Restorer,

I don't mind your expecting some recognition, little one. You deserve it! It is only natural that you should desire it.

But why do you want recognition, and from whom? That is My question.

Your happiness hinges on your answer.

Love,
Dad

Heb. 4:16　　16

Searcher,

Today I AM training you to listen. Why are you looking here for guidance?

Sing aloud for joy! Then, hear your own heart.

I inhabit your praises.

With All Wisdom and Power,
Father

I Cor. 13:4　　17

Pressured Child,

Thank you for putting up with the bull-headed, the pokey, the disorganized. Haven't you noticed My anointing?

Love,
Dad

Matt. 20:16

18

Concerned Conqueror,

The last shall be first. The first shall be last.

Why do you worry about where you'll appear in the line-up? You are already in the Kingdom, aren't you?

Yours with a Chuckle,
Father

Matt. 5:5

19

Gentle-Hearted One,

Since you don't give a hoot about who gets the best slice of turf, I AM giving you the whole territory. Oceans, continents, polar regions, forests, islands, mineral rights, mountain ranges...

How does it feel to be rich?

Love,
Dad

Ps. 78; Gal. 1:10 **20**

Baffled Liberator,

I just cannot keep everyone happy, can you? If you ever stumble across a formula for making people feel comfortable and stimulated at the same time, I'd appreciate your input.

Gotcha!

Smiling,
Dad

Matt. 4:1-11 **21**

Brave Warrior,

Satan always plots to seduce you just after you've performed exploits.

So, what else is new? To hell with the devil! Let's laugh! Our laughter annihilates lust.

Omnipotently Yours,
Dad

Jer. 9:24 **22**

Faithful Liberator,

Yes, I AM a God of exacting virtue and judgment, but above all else, I delight in mercy and kindness. And I enjoy being that way!

So few understand My nature.

Rejoicing over You Always,
Father

James 1:5 **23**

Inquiring One,

Same message I just whispered in your spirit...

Love,
Father

I Tim. 1:12-16 **24**

Trembling Child,

Don't hesitate to smile and own up to your past, when questioned. If need be, shock the self-righteous! Someone must impart hope and save searching people. Will you do it?

Your reputation rests in good hands. Mine!

> Yours with Delight,
> Dad

Rom. 6:5   **25**

Tired Conqueror,

Yes, you wavered for a moment — but have you noticed? Your lapses are growing farther apart. They are also shorter and less profound when they occur.

Your progress delights Me!

> Dad

Matt. 7:9-11   **26**

Grovelling Restorer,

Why do you feel guilty about asking Me for extras and not just necessities?

When heart priorities align with My loving purposes, I delight in fulfilling the most fleeting desires of My children.

Do you require your children to live on

weeds, worms and water? Existence *is* possible on such fare, you know...

Yours Tenderly,
Father

Luke 17:7-10; Phil. 2:5-7   **27**

Annoyed Toiler,

I know you've worked hard, and those about you appreciate your faithfulness.

So, why don't they fall prostrate at your feet in adoration?

HA!

Yours with Profound Appreciation,
Father

Ps. 143:8-10; John 16:13   **28**

Cherished Searcher,

Stop and listen! Heed your inner impressions.

The hopes and the hunches spurring you toward new ventures of faith are coming from Me. Hear Me, child. Hear Me *out*...

Helpfully,
Father

Eph. 3:20,21   **29**

Curious Child,

I know you're going to like My plans. Allow Me the pleasure of popping up with a few surprises. Do you mind?

You've asked Me to keep you flexible. I AM doing My best to accommodate...

Loving You Always,
Dad

Rom. 13:7,8   **30**

Worried One,

Not all in authority are out to get the little guy. Not all of them lust for position or power.

Ordinarily, today's bosses are yesteryear's flunkies (frightened, like yourself) scrambling to do a job nobody appreciates or wants! Can you relate?

Spectators find it easy to criticize.

Trustingly Yours,
Father

Isa. 30:18-21; Isa. 32:17,18

31

Perplexed Seeker,

Hard-liners nearly always rear children who become compromisers — or rebels.

The offspring of compromisers and rebels often lash out to become hard-liners.

Hearing My voice heals all.

Love,
Dad

.

Let's enjoy relalationship!

FEBRUARY

I Sam. 8 — 1

Diligent Disciple,

If My children name it and claim it loud and long enough, I just may let them have it. Treacherous theology, this one!

Don't you remember how the children of Israel received King Saul for their efforts?

Please, child. Let's enjoy relationship!

Love,
Dad

Mark 6:30-32 — 2

Concerned Deliverer,

Of course not! It doesn't anger Me when you grow weary of dealing with people. I understand when you become exhausted from smiling, nodding, listening. Bone tired of talking, talking, talking!

Your brain needs rest because it, too, is a part of your body. Shouldn't I know?

Your Loving Creator,
Father

Heb. 12:1-3 **3**

Sorrowful Child,

You have seen the hypocrisy of human justice. Will you now trust Me to restore your losses?

I've trusted you to endure a season of suffering, because I AM sensitizing your heart to heal shattered people.

Your Committed Ally, Always!
Father

Zeph. 3:17 **4**

Child,

Do you hear the music? At this moment I AM singing for joy over you. Thank you for caring about people.

Love,
Dad

Matt. 23:1-4 **5**

Weary One,

On occasion I lead you into the company of the stubborn, the opinionated and the adamant. Sometimes you need a refresher course that reminds you of what *not* to become.

Thank You for Trusting,
Dad

I Cor. 4:1-5   6

Weeping Warrior,

Absolute rubbish! Garbage! Slip behind the door and join Me for a chuckle when anyone nitpicks with your anointing and calling.

When you need adjustment, *I* will see to it, child. Haven't I always?

Love,
Dad

Gal. 5:6   7

Struggling Child,

Until Love establishes a track record of faithfulness, trust cannot exist, let alone flourish.

Don't worry about mustering faith, little

one. My love delights in nurturing your heart to trust.

> Faithfully, Tenderly,
> Father

Rom. 14:4,5 **8**

Child,

How does one pursue truth — uncompromising truth — and at the same time remain gentle and loving?

One must remember that he pursues Truth, not to enforce a lifestyle upon others, but to find his own healing and freedom.

> Father

Luke 15:20 **9**

Busy One,

Welcome back! I missed you.

> Love,
> Dad

---

1 John 4:10 **10**

Faithful Helper,

Thank you for lavishing love and grace

upon the undeserving and the ungrateful. That's what Life is all about, isn't It?

Yours Proudly,
Father

I John 3:20 **11**

Self-Searching Child,

Rest in My love. Be at peace. You are not playing games with My grace. If you were, I would be the First One to tell you.

Faithfully, Compassionately,
Father

Phil. 2:4-16 **12**

Penitent One,

Yes, you exploded and unloaded. I saw the pressure mounting in you long before you discovered it.

Thank you for yielding your rights to Me. Aren't you glad there's nothing left to violate?

All Is Forgiven,
Father

FEBRUARY

Ps. 100 **13**

Worshiper,

Your praises — how can I describe the joy they release in My Spirit? You make moving mountains sheer pleasure today.

Love,
Dad

Ps. 23:6 **14**

Worried Child,

Nothing about you ever bores Me. Not one bit. Your voice, your manner, your face — everything about you I find intriguing, unique and delightful.

I find nothing more boring than the lies of Our enemy! Don't you agree?

Loving You Always,
Father

Luke 7:36-50 **15**

Discouraged One,

Faithfulness is not a synonym for infallibility, little one.

I rejoice in your faithfulness. Do you know why? You keep on trying! That is what matters most, in My view.

Proudly,
Dad

II Tim. 2:13 | 16

Anguished Child,

You cannot defeat My power by dwelling in the past. You only delay its manifesting in its full glory — to your own pain.

I *will* heal the wounds of your heart.

With Deepest Compassion,
Father

Luke 10:25-37 | 17

Discerning Disciple,

Two Bible teachers eased their sedans around the blazing disaster and drove on to their "ministry" appointments.

Moments later, a male prostitute abandoned his motorbike and braved the flames

to pry a screaming toddler from the wreck-
age. Which of these three men would you
call holy?

Father

Deut. 33:27 **18**

Tender One,

Everlasting Arms enfold you. Love Indestructible surrounds you. Power Unlimited
awaits your bidding.
Hell shudders!
We smile...

Father

I Cor. 13:5,6 **19**

Beloved Truth Seeker,

Are you asking for the gift of discerning
of spirits or for the gift of fault-finding?
Heavenly discernment detects at least
two-thirds more angels than devils.
The mind of Christ is yours for the asking. Always!

Love,
Dad

Ps. 118:24 **20**

Child,

I have prepared this day for your pleasure, believe it or not.

Ask and you shall receive! Seek and you will find!

Yours Joyfully,
Father

Luke 24:44,45; II Cor. 5:13-21 **21**

Disturbed Disciple,

To understand the Bible, it must be viewed through the lenses of the four Gospels. Always!

I love you. Go back and take another look.

Tenderly,
Dad

Ps. 139:7-10 **22**

Exasperated Child,

You can leave Me if you want to. At least, you can try.

Where will you go?

Omnipresently Yours,
Father

Ps. 78 **23**

Weary Restorer,

Talk about a wild experience... Try listening to people carping because you never go out of your way to help them, when they owe their very lives to your kindness!

I Do Understand,
Father

Ps. 111:10 **24**

Child,

You're breathing now because I sustain you. I AM the King — Almighty God! Your Lord and Creator. Sometimes you forget this.

Father

Luke 1:50-53; Luke 18:10-14 **25**

Defensive One,

When you stop justifying yourself, I will justify you. I long to grant you miraculous mercy! But I can show mercy only to those who realize they need it.

I love you. That is why I tell you the truth.

Yours with Deepest Understanding,
Father

II Cor. 8:12; II Cor. 9:10 | 26

Worried Child,

The law of sowing and reaping is working for you, not against you. Which do you suppose packs the most power? The seeds of love and faith or the seeds of fear and failure?

Think about it.

With Joyful Expectancy,
Father

Jonah | 27

Determined Deliverer,

You will never do what? Say it again. I like challenges!

Love,
Father

Titus 2:14 — 28

Pressured Child,

Soon you'll laugh at any lying illusion that lures you to leave Me. Aren't you beginning to realize that I've made certain you'd find nothing to go back to?

> Yours with Commitment,
> Father

II Cor. 10:3,4; Gal. 6:6,9,10 — 29

Searching Deliverer,

If you are like I AM and yearn to see authentic Christianity thrive, dare to look to Me for guidance in your giving.

If all My children learned to do that, institutions that oppress in My Name would either purge themselves or disappear!

Love is patient. Just follow Me.

> Dad

I allow
dry seasons to spur your roots
to reach deeper into the soil of My Love.

MARCH

John 15:1   **1**

Questioning Conqueror,

Roots over-watered will rot. I allow dry seasons to spur your roots to reach deeper into the soil of My love.

Thus rooted and grounded, you will stand impervious to life's storms. Keep trusting!

I Love You,
Father

Rom. 8:35-39   **2**

Fretful One,

Nothing! Do you hear Me? Nothing in all creation ever will or ever can separate Us. Nothing!

That doesn't mean We won't have to sort through sundry problems on occasion. But I think you're worth it.

Always!

Father

MARCH

John 7:18 3

Exhausted Child,

Why do you crave popularity with people when you're popular with Me?

Nobody even begins to admire you as much as I do.

Truly!
Dad

Luke 15:1-10 4

Treasured One,

Whatever else you forget, never forget this: I love you too much to lose you!

Dad

Eph. 1:18; James 1:5 5

Deliberating One,

Are you sure this is what you want? At some point I would enjoy seeing you do something *you* actually like.

Father

Matt. 23:13; II Cor. 11:13 6

Dedicated Witness,

Which falls on your ears with greater credibility: "I love you," or "Yea verily, My soul languisheth after thee with bowels of tender mercies..."?

Hidebound religiosity hides My heart from a hurting world. Thank you for listening.

Yours Gratefully,

Father

Rom. 5:6-9 7

Searcher,

Those who refuse to receive Jesus will never find another "God" willing to die for them.

Honestly,

Dad

John 16:12 8

Faithful Warrior,

Tired minds need rest, not more information bombarding them! I have more — much more — to tell you. Many marvels, revelations and gifts await your discovery. But first you must rest. Then you will receive them as blessings and not as burdens.

Tenderly,
Dad

Ps. 131   **9**

Questioning One,

I don't mind repeating: Rest in My love! You will have to, sooner or later.
Why not begin now?

Yours Smiling,
Father

I Cor. 1:8,9   **10**

Annoyed Seeker,

Yes, you are absolutely right. I have heard your request, but I AM doing what I prefer to do anyway!
Have you thought about how often My "stubbornness" has saved you?

Yours with Eternal Devotion!
Dad

MARCH

Mark 11:25 | 11

Raging Warrior,

So you want revenge, do you? Good luck! You'll need all the luck you can get without God...

Sorrowfully,
Father

I Thess. 5:23,24 | 12

Self-Depreciating Child,

You keep putting yourself down. I keep pulling you back up. Down! Up! Down! Up!

I AM patient in this because I delight in training My little ones.

Soon you will feel more comfortable being up than down.

Love Always,
Dad

Rom. 16:20 | 13

Troubled One,

Yes, I AM angry — furious, in fact! Our

enemy will pay for this treachery.

Compassionately,
Dad

Eph. 3:20 **14**

Needy Child,

Supply will arrive soon. You can trust My reliability; just don't expect predictability.

Why do you keep looking in your mail-box?

Love,
Father

Luke 21:14,15 **15**

Trembling Liberator,

I repeat. Refuse to worry in advance how you will defend yourself.

I will give you words of wisdom that will stun your adversaries into silence!

With Pleasure!
Father

Luke 12:32 **16**

Tender One,

I was delighted to do it, child. I rejoice for your grateful heart.

Love,
Dad

Ps. 103:1-3 **17**

Cherished Child,

I love you too much to hold grudges.

Compassionately,
Dad

I Cor. 14:1; I Pet. 4:8-10 **18**

Inquisitive Conqueror,

Your quest for the supernatural — why should it offend Me? I created you to yearn for My power.

Lust for power to promote self, and despair will devour your dreams. Pursue Love, and you will perform exploits with Me!

Yours Helpfully,
Dad

Isa. 54:17 19

Weeping One,

Deliverance often arrives disguised as disaster. Will you look beyond the storm and see My salvation?

You're viewing but one time-frame in a film without end. But this drama promises pleasing outcomes for all the stories involving Our Family.

Yours with Everlasting Devotion,
Father

Josh. 2 20

Cherished Power Seeker,

I often employ disreputable-looking sources to nurture My prophets and miracle-workers. Ravens fed Elijah. Scripture reports that a prostitute once provided shelter for two men I had commissioned.

Do you want to appear respectable or to work miracles?

Father

Ps. 84:5-7; Col. 2:23 — 21

Devoted Child,

Again! Focusing on self only multiplies misery. Rest in My loving forgiveness. Return to Joy! Thus, you'll remain on My miracle-packed path of provision. It's impossible to nose-dive into clouds of doubt and despair and, at the same time, soar in the jet stream of faith.

Yours, Joyfully,

Dad

Rom. 8:26; I Cor. 2:9-13 — 22

Thirsting Truth Seeker,

I've prepared riches for you that transcend mortal imagination. My Spirit will cause you to realize, know and experience them.

Pray often in the Spirit. Release My Creative Word to carry you along the path of My provision and wisdom.

Savor supernatural surprises!

Helpfully,

Dad

Eph. 1:7,8 | 23

Searching Disciple,

How do I speak? Through all that Jesus is, represents and declares. Also, through Scripture. Through impressions. Through situations. Through experience, through nature, through people.

Sometimes hands and feet hear Me better than heads do! Enjoy living!

I AM Supporting You,
Father

Ps. 78:13-31 | 24

Indignant Disciple,

People who demand to get what they "deserve" would be shocked if I gave it to them.

But I have been known to use shock therapy as a last resort. Don't push Me.

Smiling, but Serious,
Father

MARCH

Matt. 6:25-34 | 25

Frantic Restorer,

Saving up for a rainy day? What if it never rains until the year 2187?

Consider the lilies. Think of My sparrows. Beware of battling monsters that appear only in daydreams!

Tenderly Yours,
Father

Matt. 5:6; Isa. 43:22 | 26

Blissful Adventurer,

Is it reasonable to believe that those who feel bored with Me on earth would find anything interesting about Heaven?

Missing You Terribly,
Father

II Cor. 4:6,7; Eph. 1:15-23 | 27

Worried Child,

Light exploded! Pulsating radiance showered, surrounding the tomb.

Then, two thunderbolts appeared and snapped into the shape of angels!

Awestruck, the soldiers guarding the crypt fled.

Your Lord emerged, smiling.

And you think of resurrection power as just theological rhetoric?

Have I got surprises for you!

Dad

I Cor. 4:5 **28**

Quaking Conqueror,

You weren't making up the script as you blundered your way through. A prophetic lifestyle just feels that way.

Good work!

Love,
Dad

Matt. 21:31; John 8:2-11 **29**

Learning Liberator,

I would rather live with fornicators than fault-finders. Fornicators are addicted to pleasure, and pain results as a by-product.

Fault-finders find pleasure in hurting despairing hearts — willfully!

Pleasure-addicts are easier to cure than chronic accusers. One accuser became a devil, do you recall?

Thanks for Listening,
Father

Gal. 3:28 **30**

Delightful Child,

Humans arrive in so many shapes and colors! Don't you find them interesting? Bigotry blinds. Love enlightens.

With Joy,
Father

Rom. 8:26 **31**

Deliberating Disciple,

Avoid analysis-paralysis, and savor the Supernatural! Do you realize that when you pray in the Spirit, We prophesy? When Our hearts harmonize, nothing can oppose the power of Our words!

Father

APRIL

Ps. 2:4   1

Harassed Child,

Ha! Ha! Ha! Ha! Ha! Ha! Ha! Ha! Ha! Ha! Ha! Ha! Ha! Ha! Ha! Ha! Ha! Ha! Ha! Ha! Ha! Ha! Ha! Ha!

You need to say *this* to Our enemy more often.

Yours Supportively!
Father

Ps. 63:7,8; Ps. 121:3,4   2

Child,

I AM thinking of you. Let's enjoy One Another.

Love,
Dad

Ps. 18:25-29   3

Abused and Worried One,

I outmaneuver manipulators and confront controlling personalities with their

45

error. To the crafty I show Myself shrewd. To pure hearts I show Myself faithful and mighty!

Yours, All Powerfully,
Dad

Eph. 4: 18　　　　　　　　　**4**

Trusted Deliverer,

Why take personal offense when strangers refuse to treat you with courtesy? If they saw you as a *person*, they would love you as I do.

The love-starved inhabiting our world suffer impaired vision, perceiving only human-shaped shadows.

Thanks for Understanding,
Dad

Ps. 62: 1,2; Heb. 13: 8　　　　　**5**

Weeping Child,

When all systems fail, you still have a Fail-Safe System.

Yours All Sufficiently,
Father

James 1:5,6 **6**

Inquiring Conqueror,

You've asked for My wisdom, so now you possess it. Doubting the words I've spoken to your spirit will cast you adrift upon the turbulence of human opinion.

All I ask is your trust.

Love,
Father

John 11 **7**

Frenzied One,

Don't worry about running "late" sometimes. I never do. And never have I wasted a moment!

Affectionately,
Father

Eph. 4:26 **8**

Annoyed Child,

Before you go to bed, don't forget to take out the garbage. After you take it out this time, will you keep it out?

Always at Your Disposal,
Dad

Luke 17:11-17　　　　　　**9**

Discouraged One,

Join the club! I never cease working to help My loved ones. Few ever think to say thank you.

I will reward your kindness.

Dad

Heb. 13:20　　　　　　**10**

Valiant Warrior,

Thank you for saying yes to Me and no to the evil one. You've spared not only Ourselves, but also many others from much heartache. Heaven rejoices for your courage!

Yours with Delight,
Father

Ps. 18:16-19　　　　　　**11**

Burdened Child,

Whatever power your enemies may

wield, I will free you from their tyranny!

Enjoy the spacious place I give you by grace. I help you, not because you always deserve it, but because I love you!

Always,
Your Dad

Matt. 7:6 **12**

Tender Restorer,

Exhibit honesty and integrity, yes. Adopt a policy of wholesale transparency with all people? No! Those who look to illusions for happiness resent anyone desecrating their idols.

I don't want others ripping you to shreds when you're already hurting. Lean on Me! I will deal with those who want you to replace Me for their pleasure.

Love,
Dad

Rev. 7:17 **13**

Weeping Child,

Help is on the way. I know you are hurting. It's not against the rules to cry in Our

Family.

I love kissing away tears.

Holding You Close,
Father

Ps. 33

14

Needy Child,

I spoke, and the universe sprang into existence! I merely breathed, and swirling galaxies burst into being and constellations appeared, dancing in solemn procession.

And you worry about money or the oppression of man? HA!

Confidently Yours,
Father

Phil. 1:9-11

15

Worried Peacemaker,

Bask in the serenity of My Presence. Stop analyzing past conversations and fretting about possible conflicts.

I have you covered!

Love,
Dad

APRIL

| *Zeph. 3:17; Mark 3:14* | **16** |

Cherished One,

I like you.
There, I said it again...

Dad

| *I Pet. 1:22* | **17** |

Child,

You long for purity of purpose and thought? Lavish love upon those about you! One cannot exploit and love at the same time.

Helpfully,
Father

| *Eph. 3:12,13* | **18** |

Sorrowful Stumbler,

A mad world may lock you up and throw away the key, but I hold in My possession a Key that opens all doors!

Never forget it. I have not forgotten you

for a moment. Trust My timing.

Love,
Father

Rom. 8:28 **19**

Wonderful Child,

Today you will see Me in all things — if you will look. Savor serenity! Project peace, and astonish your friends.

Always, in Joy!
Your Dad

I Cor. 2:16 **20**

Loveable Listener,

You're hearing Me right. Share the message! Boggle a mind. Win a heart.

Love,
Dad

I Thess. 5:11-15 **21**

Trusted Nurturer,

Subtle put-downs popping out, masquerading as jokes... I never find them funny. Do you?

I love showering joy and encouragement.

Always,

Your Dad

Ps. 86:1-6,15; Luke 15:20-32 **22**

Cherished Restorer,

I love you just as you are. That explains why you're seeing healing emerge in your thoughts and behavior.

All I ask is that you love others as I love you.

Ever Trusting You,

Dad

Job 42:7-10 **23**

Faithful Deliverer,

Thank you for trusting and for not giving up. Yes, you yelped and squirmed a little. So what? You stood, stubbornly trusting My Word. That's what counts!

Yours Joyfully,

Dad

Rom. 8:1,28   **24**

Weeping Warrior,

The law of life flourishing in Jesus frees you from the law of sin and destruction!

Why are you dreading backlash from your blunders? Resume walking with Me! Our fellowship will foster improved performance — in time.

Love,
Dad

Gal. 6:7-10   **25**

Beloved Child,

I love you too much to shield you from all consequences and thus warp your perception of Reality.

Dad

II Tim. 4:18   **26**

Noble Conqueror,

Everlasting life. Life indestructible! Life impervious to attack or erosion. Such life you possess forever through Jesus!

Why aren't you rejoicing?

Dad

Col. 1:9 **27**

Searching Child,

My Spirit longs to flood you with light, illuminating the eyes of your spirit to perceive My will.

Why should I play hide and seek with you? *Wanting* My will is having it!

In Joy,
Your Father

Jer. 18:1-10; I Tim. 1:18,19 **28**

Perplexed Questioner,

I did not ordain prophecy to provide a sneak preview of history before it happens.

I ordained prophecy to spur My children toward real possibilities awaiting them.

Obedience hews a path for prophecy's fulfillment.

Yours Faithfully,
Father

Matt. 23:13-15   29

Disillusioned One,

One could say that I AM addicted to authenticity — hopelessly so. The best way to escape sharing My addiction is to avoid My company. But that amounts to a full-time career, doesn't it? Never fear. Religion exists to furnish the public with the job skills to succeed!

How I rejoice that, at last, you're seeing through this silly hocus-pocus.

Truly!
Father

II Kings 6:15-17   30

Cherished Child,

My resourcefulness defies imagination!

Refuse to let appearances steal your hope. Paranoia perceives only the surface of things. Faith laughs at lying illusions!

Yours Faithfully,
Father

Remember who you are, child.
You pack astonishing power.
Use it!

MAY

Eph. 1:17-23; I John 4:4 — 1

Wavering One,

Be kind to yourself. Refuse bondage! Remember who you are, child.

You pack astonishing power. Use it!

With Joy,
Father

I Cor. 1:25 — 2

Child,

I don't mind looking ridiculous to redeem foolish people. If at times I must appear weak in the sight of the world, so be it!

My policy is to submit to crucifixion while staging a resurrection that will astound doubting minds and heal hearts.

Make friends with My policies, and enjoy exploits!

Yours Faithfully,
Father

Matt. 4:7 | 3

Wavering Warrior,

Planning an excursion? I understand. Binges explode with a vengeance in the absence of joy. Always!

Better the pleasure of sin than no pleasure at all, right?

Not really. Better to pause along the way to enjoy My flowers.

Love,
Dad

Isa. 49: 15 | 4

Treasured Child,

I love you too much to forget you.

Dad

Phil. 4:19 | 5

Worried One,

Did I promise to supply some of your needs or all of them?

MAY

Laugh at the devil's double talk!
I do!

Father

James 4:7   **6**

Pressured Restorer,

Devils just will not submit to reason! Why do you think Heaven gave them the boot?

You do likewise!

Yours, All Powerfully,
Dad

II Tim. 1:12   **7**

Weeping Child,

I keep *all* you commit to My care.

Heaven harbors unexpected treasures that are guaranteed to astound many.

Faithfully Yours,
Father

II Cor. 12:9,10   **8**

Frustrated Trooper,

I knew exactly what I was getting into when I chose you!

In your weakness My strength is made perfect. Keep walking.

Yours Faithfully,
Father

James 2:12,13   **9**

Inquiring Disciple,

Mercy triumphs over judgment! This means love throws a party when people don't have to pay through the nose for their blunders.

What inspires you to celebrate? Just asking...

Love,
Father

Ps. 78:40-42   **10**

Perplexed Pioneer,

I engineered your escape. Why are you still unhappy? Pull your mind into the present.

Faithfully,
Father

Ps. 46:10 11

Devoted Truth Seeker,

Constant drilling into "deep issues" makes for a boring mind. Can't We just hug sometimes?

Remember the rubbing-off effect of My Presence.

Yours Joyfully — Always,
Dad

Rom. 14:10 12

Curious One,

I refuse even to address your suspicions. Another's frailties are none of your business!

I enjoy singing, not snooping. Any more questions?

Yours with Fierce Loyalty,
Father

Luke 16:15 13

Inquiring Disciple,

Long faces, dark colors, somber voices intoning pious-sounding noises... Do you find them impressive?

Personally, I prefer watching Bugs Bunny.

I'm serious!

Father

I John 3:20   **14**

Conscientious Conqueror,

Avoid the snare of morbid introspection! I have redeemed your yesterdays and will guard your tomorrows.

Instead of making rash vows, just remember My vows to you. Heaven celebrates your progress!

Father

Ps. 34:8; I Cor. 4:20   **15**

Tired Disciple,

Overloaded with opinions? Befuddled by too many words and formulas bombarding your mind? Tired of hearing teaching, teaching, and more teaching?

Good! At last you're realizing that nothing can replace the sheer joy of My Presence, of experiencing My Essence!

Expectantly,
Father

II Cor. 10:3-5 **16**

Daring Deliverer,

Experience explodes arguments! Miracles unravel clever reasoning and spur people to re-evaluate their ideologies.

Put on the mind of Christ, and dare to listen to your heart! Let's astonish a few doubters today — not excluding yourself.

All Is Forgiven,
Father

Prov. 2:8 **17**

Stymied Child,

No one is wasting your time. I interrupted your schedule for a progress report. You look ten years younger with your pulse rate back to normal!

Truly,
Father

Phil. 3:2,15   18

Striving Child,

Scrub, polish, alter, whack and chisel on your personality all you wish! Only My love can birth healing and holiness.

Father

Ps. 105:3-7; I Thess. 5:18   19

Treasured Trooper,

Today you're learning the secret of savoring contentment in every situation.
Delightful, isn't it?

Love,
Dad

Isa. 53   20

Broad-Minded Explorer,

Jesus just *is* the Way, the Truth and the Life. Why? I cannot translate to human beings what I AM all about without Jesus! Ordinary people would find it impossible to relate to a

God that never got bumps and bruises.

Love,
Dad

Prov. 3:5,6 **21**

Searching One,

Today's revelation? Keep walking.

I AM!
Father

Rom. 2:1-6 **22**

Treasured Restorer,

Nearly everyone wants a God of grace for themselves, yet they demand a God of judgment for others!

Child, where do you stand on this issue?

Yours Faithfully,
Father

Prov. 16:32 **23**

Seething Servant,

Sorry everything and everyone annoys you right now. It's an interesting challenge for Omnipresence — but I'm doing My best to stay out of your way!

Of course, when you need Me, I AM always available.

> Protecting You Always,
> Dad

Ps. 37:34,39,40 | 24

Shaken Conqueror,

It's not too late to start again. Enter into praise, and refuse to look back. Refuse to let appearances erode your resolve or plunder your peace.

This time you will go in *My* power. HA! Do you realize Our enemies are already scrambling for cover?

> Yours with Renewed Mercies,
> Father

Matt. 6:7,8 | 25

Frustrated One,

I AM not deaf. I'm just waiting for you to finish talking.

> Yours Respectfully,
> Father

Ps. 144:1 26

Impatient Conqueror,

Rely on My loving wisdom and trust My timing. If I enjoyed seeing you suffer, I would scrap preparation and grant you promotion — as requested!

What kind of father do you imagine Me to be?

Yours Compassionately,

Dad

Eph. 2:8-10; Col. 2:9 27

Fretful Child,

Stop reviewing your track record and choose to review Mine. You can never score high enough to earn My favor and blessings. They are already yours!

As I have told you, it is not your manipulation but My mercy that moves mountains.

Just to adjust your thinking...

Lovingly,

Father

James 2:12,13   28

Little One,

Opinionated personalities who never cease trying to alter others will find themselves isolated. Who can fault folks for dreading their company?

How tragic that self-appointed purgers experience such loneliness! Yet, how fortunate are those who escape their tyranny...

Yours with a Heavy Heart,
Dad

Phil. 4:5   29

Inquiring Liberator,

A bath in boric acid or an atmosphere bristling with toxic criticism — which is worse?

Blessed are the encouragers!

Yours Trustingly,
Father

Num. 22:27-34 | 30

Busy One,

How was it that the prophet Balaam's she-ass possessed greater prophetic powers than did her master?

The pure in heart shall see God. Ambitious minds miss miracles!

We need to discuss priorities.

Yours Helpfully,
Father

Matt. 5:9 | 31

Courageous Child,

My peacemakers act as blessed shock-absorbers in this world. They bear the brunt of the blows exchanged between the raging and the ruthless.

Now you know how I feel. It hurts, doesn't it? Loving people who detest one another...

Expect rewards that will raise some envious eyebrows!

Yours Proudly,
Dad

My all-knowing
heart needs no
explanation.

JUNE

I Pet. 5:7 **1**

Heavy-Hearted One,

Anything you long to express, I long to hear. Or you can just cry as I hold you in My arms, if you want to.

My all-knowing heart needs no explanation.

Tenderly,
Father

Heb. 11:6 **2**

Baffled Deliverer,

Do you want bewilderment bombarding your mind for a lifetime? Then solicit everyone's opinion — about everything! Teeter on a tightrope for people who couldn't care less and for those who are impossible to please!

When I speak, refuse to respond until 10,000 confirmations arrive, hand-delivered by angels!

Yours with Tender Concern,
Father

John 14:26,27 — 3

Child,

I love you too much to let you live in illusion.

Dad

Luke 2:36-38 — 4

Worried One,

It is nonsense to fear aging, because everyone *will* grow older.

Has it occurred to you that every stage of life offers unique advantages and privileges?

The Ancient of Days,
Your Dad

Matt. 11:28-30 — 5

Weary Warrior,

Right. Loving Me is one thing; putting up with people is another!

Or so it seems to your jangled nerves at the moment. Will you pause and receive My refreshment?

With Deepest Understanding,
Dad

JUNE

Isa. 55:11   **6**

Faithful Restorer,

I never go back on My Word! Aren't you glad? I knew you would be. Treat others as I treat you. I will help you.

With Deepest Trust,
Father

Matt. 5:38-42   **7**

Generous Child,

Reckon it as a gift offered to Me, and you will no longer feel robbed or plundered.

What is given to Me remains with Me. Have you forgotten We are Family?

I Love You,
Father

James 2:14-17   **8**

Child,

Sometimes a square meal helps more than a revelation. Love people! Some are hurting too much to make heads or tails of theology.

Yours Trustingly,
Dad

John 16:21   **9**

Treasured One,

Just to confirm... You are on the brink of a breakthrough! Not a breakdown, but a breakthrough.

Birth pains often feel like death pangs, weary one. You needn't strive. I AM holding you, protecting you, guiding you.

Faithfully!
Father

Matt. 10:7-10   **10**

Tender One,

I forgive you. Now go, not to get, but to give. I approve you, receive you and delight to support you.

You journey, not to be affirmed, but to impart hope and healing.

Always,
Your Father

James 4:1-7 **11**

Stressed Inquirer,

People intimidate and control because they fall prey to a spirit of fear. Paranoia breeds power struggles, accusation and slander.

Rest in My love, child. Resign from the rat race! Trust Me to restore and vindicate.

Imploringly,
Father

Luke 15:11-24 **12**

Tearful Rescuer,

Sometimes Love must allow others to live with their choices. Is it merciful to deny people the wealth born of experience?

Please, child. Learn to relax a little more, trusting My Holy Spirit! I will watch over your loved ones.

Yours Tenderly *and* Resourcefully,
Dad

Luke 4:18,19; I Pet. 3:8,9 | **13**

Recovering Child,

All I ask is that you choose to forgive, and I will help you forget.

You're doing your part. Thank you for trusting while I'm doing Mine.

You will not always suffer this pain.

With Deepest Compassion and Respect,
Father

John 8:15; John 9:1-3 | **14**

Inquiring Restorer,

A near-suicide victim encased in splints and plaster doesn't need to hear rebuke for having violated natural law or morality! Hurting people need healing.

Thank you for imparting hope to despairing hearts. So many accuse and point fingers! So few comfort and heal.

Yours Trustingly,
Father

Acts 10:25,26   **15**

Willing Nurturer,

I love you too much to let others mistake you for Me. Aren't you glad?

Always Your Ally,
Father

Titus 3:1-5   **16**

Raging Restorer,

I respect you. Therefore I grant you enormous freedom of thought and expression — even when you're dead wrong!

Will you deny others the same freedom?

Yours Smiling,
Father

Phil. 3:12-15   **17**

Dear Child,

How do My mature children evaluate success? They define success as "sanctified stubbornness"! They freely admit their frailty while refusing to allow past failures to haunt them. Their dreams drive them on toward their destinies.

I think you're growing up!

Yours Proudly,
Father

I Cor. 1:4-9; I Cor. 13:8-12 | 18

Searching One,

Who said that miracles ceased after the death of the last apostle? I didn't!

Don't cheat yourself...

Yours with a Grin,
Father

John 14:27 | 19

Treasured Child,

My Son has given you peace that the world can neither offer nor steal.

Don't allow *anyone* to talk you out of it.

Yours with All Power,
Father

II Cor. 9:8-10 **20**

Tender-Hearted One,

This will not be the last time you empty your pockets. Isn't living by faith stimulating?

Proudly Your Provider,
Father

Isa. 30:15 **21**

Child,

Do you feel your liver, your pancreas, your cerebral cortex or thyroid?

Why do you struggle to feel My Presence? It's time you made friends with My Personality. I enjoy quietness. Strength surges and faith flourishes in quietness.

Forever Yours with Confidence,
Father

I John 1:9 **22**

Self-Scrutinizing One,

Forget the past. Rejoice in My love. Focus on now — and be happy!

Heaven desires it. I command it. You deserve it!

Dad

II Cor. 4:6,7 **23**

Desperate Petitioner,

I AM here. Why are you shouting?

Father

James 1:17,18 **24**

Cherished Child,

I AM not the author of confusion or fear. Return to fellowship with Me, and walk on!

Do you recall that every good and perfect gift comes from the Father of Lights? Yes, and you, child, are one of My lights. Your radiance threatens Our enemy...

Wonderful!

Dad

I John 5:21 **25**

Steadfast Disciple,

Idolatry betrays its presence through inflexibility. Worshiping inanimate gods turns hearts into stone or metal.

It doesn't anger Me that you resist change, little one. All I AM asking is *why* do you fear it? Think about it.

With Liberating Love,
Father

Ps. 144:1,2 26

Child,

I love you too much to spare you from growing pains.

With Deepest Affection,
Father

II Cor. 1:20 27

Mighty Conqueror,

You are healed. All symptoms are fading. Beware of doubt and cynicism! Those devils lurk in the shadows of negative analysis, just looking for ways to devour your joy.

Yours Everlastingly,
Dad

II Tim. 1:9 | 28

Weary Warrior,

Will you cease striving to become worthy of Me? Please, child. My Son has made you worthy forever.

Our enemy delights in seducing My children into spending their lifetimes toiling for what I've already given them!

Yours Tenderly,
Father

Eph. 5:8-11 | 29

Trusted Trooper,

I created you to conquer. Just remember who you are! View every trial as an invitation to experience the miraculous — as a door opening into supernatural exploits of power!

All Sufficiently Yours,
Father

Psalms 15

30

Searching One,

I enjoy the scenario of theater and costume as much as anyone does!

But does reverence consist of donning old-fashioned clothes, talking shoddy Shakespearean, and tiptoeing about in cadence with organ music?

HA! Thou waxeth too old to buy into that blarney. Love people! Eshew pomposity.

Yea, Verily!
Thy Dad

Yes,
it appears you
and I are stuck with
One Another;
I Am not complaining
about it, are you?

JULY

John 6:37 — 1

Relieved Wanderer,

Yes, it appears that you and I are stuck with One Another. I AM not complaining about it, are you?

Yours with Deepest Delight,
Dad

Isa. 41:10 — 2

Treasured Restorer,

Refuse to fear, for I AM with you. Do not despair, for I AM your God. I will strengthen you and I will help you. I will uphold you with My righteous right hand. Even now I AM fulfilling these words!

Faithfully!
Father

Matt. 11:28,29 — 3

Frantic Freedom Fighter,

No man is busier than the one protecting

his "rights." You look exhausted today.

Ever Thinking of You,
Father

Ps. 68: 1-3   **4**

Awakening Warrior,

Tired of being victimized? Rebel against hell! Dare to resume pursuing Our dreams. Spend today's remaining hours terrifying satan!

Enjoy freedom! Celebrate your independence from bondage! Shatter the shadowy shackles of worry and false guilt with laughter.

Triumphantly!
Father

Ps. 147:10,11   **5**

Unrelenting Restorer,

Refusing rest makes the mind vulnerable to vices. Seduction loves to entrap My trustworthy workers by whispering, "break time!"

I would weep seeing you broken.

Yours with Tender Concern,
Father

I Kings 19:11,12 — 6

Cherished Child,

You perceive My signals more often than you think. Why do I whisper? Your spirit yearns for the serenity of Mine.

With Strength Everlasting,
Father

John 5:19; I Pet. 2:21-23 — 7

Browbeaten Child,

Do you want to know how to nudge chronic critics over the edge? Dare to smile kindly and remain silent! Reply *only* if I clearly lead you to speak.

Jesus did this, and did He raise a ruckus! Redemption resulted.

Helpfully,
Father

James 3:17 — 8

Zealous Child,

My wisdom submits to honest inquiry and always delights in showing mercy, with patience.

Does yours?

I Love Helping You,
Father

Acts 10:9-28 **9**

Bold Deliverer,

Just another warning. Never say never *unless* you're dying to do it.

Yours Chuckling,
Father

I Kings 19:11,12; I Cor. 2:15 **10**

Noble Conqueror,

Take courage! My thoughts are now your thoughts. So, your thoughts (ordinary as they may feel) are indeed coming from Me.

Enjoy exploits!

Powerfully Yours,
Father

John 15:15 **11**

Child of My Heart,

I will tell you again. I don't mind telling

you again and again — and yet again. I LIKE YOU.

That does a number on your theology, doesn't it?

Good!

Dad

I Sam. 3:1-14; Ezek. 22:30 **12**

Trusted Warrior,

My heart is aching. Do you mind if I cry on your shoulder for a few moments? I know this would sound silly to many people. Intercession attracts few in Our Household.

Sorrowfully,
Father

Neh. 8:10; I Thess. 5:16 **13**

Worried One,

Satan does *not* share equal power with Me! Evil is a parasite. Our laughter can dislodge it in an instant, have you noticed?

Love,
Dad

I Thess. 4:13-18

14

Concerned Inquirer,

The evangelicals are right. *Jesus is coming!* But Scripture says to comfort one another with these words, not to terrify one another with these words!

More dreadful by far would loom the prospect of living in a dying world without any such hope for the future.

Gently, Helpfully,
Father

Ps. 18:2-6; Isa. 59:19

15

Tortured Child,

Those dark daydreams that rage in your mind are not yours. Why should I be angry with *you*? Those lying illusions come from Our enemy! He's hoping to make you forget who you are. Child, sometimes you may forget, but I never will. Not in a million eternities! Not ever!

Your Mighty Fortress,
Father

Num. 6:25 **16**

Tired Trooper,

Expect strength to surge within you as you go, trusting in Me.

I can pack the benefits of twelve hours of sleep into two. No problem! Dare to arise, singing!

Love,
Dad

Gen. 1:26,27 **17**

Ruthless Reasoner,

If your brain cells evolved from random atoms colliding in an irrational universe, why does your mind detest other such collisions like mass genocide, torture and stealing? Did a cosmic "accident" produce those marvels called human reason and conscience?

Couldn't resist asking!

Ever Pursuing You,
Father

I Kings 19:3-18; John 4:4-11 18

Sulking Restorer,

Are you angry with Me? Why? Because I neglected to solicit your opinion concerning My plans?

Surely you're not serious...

Yours Chuckling,
Almighty God

Eph. 6:4 19

Tender One,

Do you think I would admonish fathers not to browbeat their children and yet live contrary to My own counsel?

Test the spirits! My Spirit never shackles people to shame.

Love,
Dad

John 1:9-11 20

Dear Child,

Reality exterminates myths. By its very nature, truth scoffs at trivia by showing it up as the sham that it is.

Child, do you expect to reflect My Light and live free of flak at the same time?

Jesus couldn't!

Yours with Deepest Understanding,
Father

Matt. 8:22 **21**

Reliable Restorer,

Their problem is not your problem — not unless you insist on making it yours!

Relish rest. You need it.

Tenderly,
Father

Eph. 2:4-7 **22**

Wonderful Warrior,

My Son suffered untold agony to enthrone you in the highest of all positions. Why do you keep putting yourself down?

Respectfully,
Father

Ps. 121:3-8   **23**

Treasured Child,

Has it occurred to your mind that I don't know how to forget you?

Sometimes I weep when you worry.

With Tender Concern,

Father

II Cor. 3:16-18; Col. 2:20-23   **24**

Analyzing Liberator,

To focus on self is to succumb to the tyranny of mind-binding despair. Can hell's reign cause the flower of virtue to flourish?

Repent of scorning yourself, and look only to Me. Only Love nurtures hearts into wholeness.

Devoted to You Always,

Dad

John 15:14   **25**

Inquiring Seeker,

No, I AM not losing patience. I've spoken words of life to your heart again and again.

And I will continue to do so! But, sooner or later you must *respond* to My words. Those who hear them can enjoy their benefit only if they heed them.

Always Your Friend,
Father

Matt. 6:7,8 **26**

Chosen Child,

The sound of your voice delights Me. I like hearing you talk.

When you pray, why do you wrestle with words, cherished one? It is the accuser who nitpicks with your vocabulary, not I. I AM hearing your heart.

Always!
Dad

Ps. 18:31-34 **27**

Anxious One,

Are you running scared? Trembling? Covering bases? Rehearsing defenses?

Stop! My glory shields you and My love

secures you, little one. I will *not* abandon you.

Rest in My Embrace,
Father

Ps. 32:8-11 **28**

Child,

You're on the right track. Keep tracking with Me. I AM tracking with you.

Love,
Dad

Eph. 4:1-6 **29**

Racing Restorer,

Remember! I work over all, through all, and in all. When you slam doors and mutter and stomp, who are you raging against?

Don't plunge into guilt. Just stop!

Please...
Father

Matt. 6:19-24 **30**

Beloved Conqueror,

Expect supply to arrive soon! When the

money rolls in, what will happen to Us?
A penny for your thoughts...

Yours Affectionately,
Father

Isa. 53:4,5

31

Child,

Jesus carried your sorrows. He bore your wounds, absorbing your sins and their dread harvest into His innocence. His stripes replaced the searing pain of your sickness with His wholeness.

Cherished one, why do you plead for My mercy? You have it.

With Love Everlasting,
Father

I PUT THORNS IN THE NEST
TO NUDGE THEM OUT
INTO DISCOVERY.

AUGUST

Isa. 40:27-30

Learning Liberator,

Those who shy away from My power are like young eagles that shy away from soaring. They have yet to understand their identities and destinies.

I put thorns in the nest to nudge them out into discovery. Exciting, isn't it?

Yours Chuckling,
Father

John 13:7

Inquiring Listener,

I know. You cannot understand what I AM doing right now. But you will understand later on. Trust Me! I AM leading you into deliverance, not destruction.

You are My handiwork, My creation, My treasure!

Love,
Dad

Eph. 3:20   **3**

Child,

I love you too much to say yes to all your requests.

Dad

Gal. 4:15-31   **4**

Pressured Conqueror,

What happened to all your joy? Beware of joy-killers, popping in out of nowhere and annihilating liberty in "Jesus' Name."

Such ministries only spread misery in a world already despairing of hope.

Loving You Always,
Dad

Heb. 6:10   **5**

Tender One,

Yours is a heart overflowing with kindness for others. When you need mercy, do you think I will reward your gentleness with punishment? Unthinkable!

Love,
Father

II Cor. 4:7 | 6

Disillusioned Disciple,

No one could live with you if you appeared too perfect in your own sight. Not even I could live with you, child.

My glory best reveals itself through rough-hewn humanity, which Scripture calls "vessels of clay." Has it occurred to you that you just may qualify?

Yours Cheerfully,
Father

I John 5:21 | 7

Grieving Child,

My heart aches for your sorrow. I didn't laugh when your idol fell from its pedestal.

I regret the grief idolatry has caused you. Consider it a violent rescue.

With Deepest Devotion,
Dad

Ps. 56 **8**

Little One,

I know your pain. I cry with you. Lean on Me. Refuse to confuse Our enemy's work for Mine.

I AM your Rock of Refuge.

> **Always!**
> Dad

Ps. 23 **9**

Bewildered Searcher,

Berserk as it appears, you are on the right path. You should see the ones I spared you from walking!

> Dad

Matt. 26:6-13 **10**

Weary Worker,

When you know you've done your very best, don't allow carping critics to destroy your joy.

Trust Me to call all nitpickers to task. I will!

Yours Faithfully,
Father

Heb. 5:7,8 **11**

Questioning Restorer,

Why did I allow you to suffer betrayal? Now you know how *never* to treat a friend.

I trusted you in that trial.

With Deepest Compassion,
Father

Heb. 13:14-16 **12**

Tired Restorer,

One can never do enough to satisfy a nit-picker! Some people just prefer hell over Happiness.

Not so with you!

Joyfully,
Father

Luke 7:36-50 | 13

Weeping Child,

Peace, tender one. Those who size you up and stuff you in a slot labeled "sinner" will find themselves dealing with Me.

Hide and watch! Enjoy refuge in Our Hiding Place. Do you remember His Name? Jesus is your Strong Deliverer.

Always,
Father

Gal. 3:1-14 | 14

Meticulous Trooper,

Qualifying yourself for Heaven by keeping rules? Fine! Just make sure that you keep them *all*. And all for all the *right reasons*, too.

What joy! Striving to be 100 percent right, every second of every minute of every hour of every day of every week of every month of every year of every decade... Right? Wrong. Damnable perfection, this!

Father

Rom. 3:23,24 | 15

Conscientious Child,

Don't demand perfection from people and you'll not be disappointed. Just expect daily signs and wonders from Me.

Joyfully,
Father

Gal. 6:1-5,7 | 16

Loving Liberator,

Sometimes My mercy arrives as judgment. Could I be merciful and let evil reign unrestrained in your world?

Just allow Me to do the judging.

Many Thanks!
Father

Heb. 10:35,36 | 17

Questioning One,

I AM more interested in your healing than today's happiness.

You're not the only one who thinks I'm "too slow."

> Yours Patiently,
> Dad

Titus 2:11-14 **18**

Child of My Joy,

Arise in the Anointing! Say no to temptation and watch it wither away. Better yet, say yes to My Spirit. Hell seeks another platform when it loses the limelight of center stage.

> Helpfully,
> Dad

Phil. 2:12,13 **19**

Perplexed Child,

Why are you waiting on Me? I AM waiting on you!

> Ever Supporting You,
> Father

Rom. 15:7 **20**

Treasured Restorer,

Aren't you glad I look beyond your behavior, beholding your pain and your weakness?

All I ask is that you do the same for others. I will help you.

Yours Faithfully,
Father

Matt. 11:19   **21**

Holy Helper,

Holiness overlooks crude words and loves people! It scorns the somber sanctimony and sham of religion. True holiness laughs!

Through your love and laughter, can your fellow workers even detect that I like them?

Just asking...

Father

II Chron. 20:15; II Cor. 1:20   **22**

Little One,

Stand still, and behold My deliverance! This battle is not yours, but Mine.

Your Almighty Defender,
Dad

Eph. 6:17,18 **23**

Tireless Trooper,

I know. You long to help people, not hurt them. Learn to trust My still small voice, and enjoy awe-inspiring protection and wisdom.

I've noted your sacrifices.

Proudly,
Dad

James 4:6 **24**

Terse Child,

Pouting keeps everyone guessing, doesn't it? Furious work done in quiet rage with tight lips makes people tremble and walk softly!

And you are demanding that I grant you *more* authority...?

HA!
Father

II Pet. 1:3 — 25

Concerned Conqueror,

Yes, I agree. Knowledge is power. Therefore, you possess power — unlimited power! Your knowledge of Me (not *about* Me, but *of* Me) grants you the wealth of infinite wisdom and might.

You are not a victim. Your natural liabilities are My opportunities. Stop worrying!

Love,
Dad

Matt. 13:11-16 — 26

Searching Disciple,

I have blessed your eyes with supernatural vision and your ears with miraculous hearing. Will you dare to use them?

Trust Me to cover and guide you. Rigid religiosity results from refusing to trust.

Always Your Rock of Refuge,
Father

Ps. 145 **27**

Child,

Peace... What is it? Peace is what happens when My children choose to believe that I AM ALL-POWERFUL!

> Your Almighty Father

Col. 2:8,9 **28**

Exhausted Child,

How can one detect the absence of true holiness? By the presence of any oppression exterminating hope, simplicity, trust.

Beware! Grace exterminators usually arrive disguised as proclaimers of "holiness."

> Helpfully,
> Father

John 13:8 **29**

Child,

I will never change My mind about you. I think you're wonderful! Too wonderful to leave alone.

Sorry you find this irksome at times.

> Dad

Ps. 16:11 **30**

Diligent Disciple,

I like laughter! One can always find Me rollicking in the midst of it.

Some people never will find Me. I keep looking for them anyway.

Always in Joy,
Your Dad

John 14:6; Rom. 1:16,17 **31**

Recovering Restorer,

I AM the Higher Power for which you are searching. If you long to know what I AM like, observe Jesus!

Read the Gospels in a modern translation. Scrap religious tradition and dare to open your mind.

And be prepared — for miracles!

Yours Everlastingly,
Father

I often link "neatness freaks"

and "sloppy slouches" together...

SEPTEMBER

Rom. 11:33-36; I Cor. 12:21-26　　**1**

Beleaguered Deliverer,

I often link "neatness freaks" and "sloppy slouches" together to heal them.

Don't you find My wisdom delightful?

Dad

Isa. 66:5　　**2**

Tender One,

I know. You sought counsel and received condemning judgment instead. People scorned your weakness and exploited your pain. Foolish mortals!

Pray for them, child. Your betrayers must learn mercy the hard way. I promise you! They *will* learn.

With Deepest Compassion,
Dad

SEPTEMBER

Matt. 10:24,25   **3**

Struggling Shepherd,

You have My approval. Why do you demand universal acceptance? Not even I enjoy that.

Yours with a Smile,
Father

James 4: 7,8   **4**

Pressured Child,

Lust withers and dies under the healing light of My love.
Draw near!

Father

I Cor. 13:6,7   **5**

Child,

Are you a Christian?
Test: When another person falters, do you spread the word or do you weep?
I just want you to determine whose side you are on.

Love,
Dad

116

II Cor. 10:1-5 6

Child,

Rationalization unravels when revelation arrives, boggling minds with amazing miracles!

Stop rehearsing arguments! Why fight fire with fire when you possess the Atomic "Balm"?

Your Strong Defense,
Father

Matt. 14:25-32 7

Weary One,

Start again! Call the other attempts practice. I have all of the time in all worlds for you, child.

Yours with Eternal Commitment,
Father

Matt. 18:21,22 8

Bruised Child,

My children will never feel secure in My love until they know I walk what I talk.

Forgiving seventy times seven daily was My idea.

Tenderly,
Your Dad

Ps. 103: 8/4 **9**

Loveable Child,

Forgiveness is an act of the will. My will inclines toward forgiveness. Aren't you grateful?

Then please align your will with Mine.

Many Thanks,
Father

Heb. 12:5,6 **10**

Frustrated Child,

I only "hassle" the people I love. Do you think I enjoy scrambling the schedules of My squawking children?

I AM bailing you out. Consider yourself rescued! Your trust would be appreciated...

Love,
Dad

Ps. 131; I Cor. 1:30,31

11

Frantic Scrambler,

Make friends with your mortality, and you will transcend it. Embrace your limitations as allies, and you will expand them.

Peace arrives only when warring ceases. You possess Wisdom and Life Everlasting! Why battle for what is already yours?

Forever through Jesus,
Father

Luke 10:41

12

Harassed Housekeeper,

Which do you prefer: Messy houses filled with laughter and love? Or tidy dwellings inhabited by uptight people? In My view, the better homes and gardens are the user-friendly ones.

Suit yourself!

Yours Chuckling,
Dad

Acts 11:1-18 13

Bewildered Liberator,

Yes, I open some doors leading into paths you would avoid if you knew about them in advance.

Often your enrichment depends on your investment in others. Trust Me! Do you have any other choice?

Yours Faithfully, Proudly!
Father

Prov. 3:3,4 14

Weary One,

Keep on loving, forgiving and showing mercy. I do! Where would anyone be if I didn't?

All Powerfully Yours,
Dad

I John 1:9 15

Child,

Don't allow remorse to drive you away

from My Presence. Give hell no reason to
celebrate!

Tenderly,
Father

John 15:12   **16**

Zealous Child,

An explosion waiting to happen; "hell on
wheels" some people called you. Yet I won
your heart with My tenderness, didn't I?

What do you mean you want Me to teach
them a lesson? Clarification, please...

Dad

Matt. 6:7,8   **17**

Fervent One,

I don't mind your repeating yourself, if
you find it helpful. But when you reach a
stopping place, will you pause and allow Me
to reply?

Many Thanks,
Father

SEPTEMBER

Acts 16:6,7

18

Frustrated Adventurer,

So? You explored another blind alley. Nothing builds one's experience like exploration! Unless it's doing the same things over and over and over and over and...

Affectionately,
Father

Acts 9:1-19

19

Faithful Child,

Many people who scoff at the idea of modern-day miracles will change their minds — sooner or later. Desperation provokes re-evaluation.

Yours with a Chuckle,
Dad

Ps. 34:1-10

20

Searcher,

I shield you every step of the way. Angels emitting blazing brilliance surround you, protecting your path.

Have you seen them? Open wide the eyes of your spirit, and behold!

Yours with Devotion,
Father

Acts 16:16-34 **21**

Bewildered Deliverer,

Sometimes I let you muddle into messes to show you miracles. I AM saving you from stagnation and liberating you from boredom.

Exciting, isn't it?

Love,
Dad

Hab. 2:18,19 **22**

Child,

I love you too much to let idolatry destroy you.

Dad

Col. 2:23; Col. 3:1-3 **23**

Dedicated Disciple,

Harboring anger against self only stifles faith and fosters more failure.

My children live by faith, not self-flagellation! Ease up, little one. If only you knew My tender heart toward you...

Yours Compassionately,
Father

II Tim. 2:13 **24**

Cherished One,

Your feelings fluctuate, but My love never fails. Never, never, never!

Yours with Solid Commitment,
Dad

I Pet. 5:10,11 **25**

Weary One,

I know it hasn't been easy for you. Heaven applauds your patience!

With Profound Understanding,
Father

I Pet. 2:2 **26**

Perplexed Perfectionist,

You lived on earth about a year before you began toddling. Do you think I expect you to sprout wings and soar with angels by next summer?

I AM pleased with your progress! Let's enjoy One Another.

Love,
Dad

I Sam. 17:41-51 | 27

Child,

Refuse to let any person or power intimidate you. Don't worry about what you don't have to give.

Give what you have. I AM Love. You have Me. Always!

Father

Ps. 139:1-10; 23,24 | 28

Exasperated One,

So you think I always get My own way, do you? I've noticed it hasn't hampered you much.

Count your blessings!

Love,
Father God

John 3:16 29

Child,

I regard *you* as more than ample reward for My efforts. Isn't it caring for people that counts, more than anything else in life?

I'm glad We agree.

Love Always,
Dad

I Cor. 1:20-25; I Cor. 15:1-8 30

Deep Thinker,

You are right. Like a loose bolt banging around in the works, so the Man, Jesus, clatters in the machinery of materialistic philosophy. Why do you think I sent Him?

A well-documented resurrection has a way of unraveling naturalism.

We'll talk again...

Father

For heaven's sake lighten up! Will you?

OCTOBER

Matt. 6:16-18 · 1

Intense Trooper,

Some people fall into a fallacy. They project a public image far more serious than Mine!

I love children — noise, wiggles and all. I enjoy a good joke and find dancing delightful. And just think — how will long-faced religionists react when they find animals in Heaven!?

For Heaven's sake, lighten up! Will you?

Yours Joyfully,
Father

Matt. 12:18-21; II Tim. 2:13 · 2

Recovering Child,

A bruised reed He will not break, a smouldering candle He will not snuff out...

Jesus is the Light of Life; therefore, My Son perfectly reflects My nature! Why do you tremble in fear of My wrath?

I AM working to fulfill your dearest dreams — to heal you, not to abuse you.

Tenderly,
Father

Ps. 14　　　　　　　　　**3**

Beloved Searcher,

People who view human life as a cosmic accident will live by that view — sooner or later!

Pity those who have to live with them.

Your Mighty Fortress,
Father God

I Tim. 6:6-16　　　　　　**4**

Puzzled Conqueror,

I know you will enjoy real security when you abandon all illusions. Thus, I let this world and all its systems disillusion you, little by little. My miracle-workers just cannot invest their hopes in lost causes!

Love,
Dad

Luke 22:31-34

5

Chosen Child,

I know all about you, and I AM still here. Doesn't this say anything to you?

Father

Gal. 5:22,23

6

Child,

What is the secret of keeping people frantic? Scurrying to please?

Cultivate hypersensitivity! Interpret the smallest oversight as a personal affront!

Enjoy solitude — for a lifetime.

Yours with Tender Concern,

Father

Matt. 5:41

7

Faithful One,

Thank you for going an extra mile!

Now you've got them wondering what in Heaven's NAME you're up to!

HA!

Dad

II Cor. 5:16 **8**

Loveable Listener,

"It's not the money, it's the principle! It's not their odd and frumpy clothing, it's the principle! It's not that I'm a racist, it's the principle! I'm not judging, it's just the principle!"

Intolerance, hatred, bigotry, envy and greed find enormous satisfaction in preaching "principles."

I AM not impressed. Are you?

Father

Ps. 78:11-17 **9**

Beloved Searcher,

Do you really think you'd find it easier to exercise faith if I kept bombarding you with miracles?

Why didn't My multiplied miracles cause faith to flourish in the Israelites who followed Moses in the wilderness?

Ingratitude devours trust. What a monster!

Helpfully,
Father

I Pet. 2:23,24 10

Dear Child,

When criticized, receive it as an opportunity to perceive the pain of another's heart. If guilty, repent. If not, rejoice that Jesus trusted you to share in His suffering and Mine.

Dad

II Thess. 3:7-10 11

Concerned Conqueror,

Your fellow workers don't expect perfection from you. You'll be amazed by how just showing basic reliability will impress them! It takes time to establish a track record.

Keep up the good work!

All Powerfully Yours,
Father

Lam. 3:22-26 12

Cherished Child,

Mercy! Just think for a moment. What incredible kindness I shower upon you daily!

Is there any reason why today should be different?

Yours Grinning,
Father

Heb. 4:14-16; James 4:7 | 13

Weary Restorer,

No. I never grow tired of hauling you out of ditches, little one. You're the one who becomes weary, not I.

I do look forward to your enjoying another lifestyle. Soon you'll become tired enough of this one to opt for a new one.

I Remain Yours, Patiently,
Father

II Tim. 1:12 | 14

Beloved Searcher,

You know Me now! You understand My heart and My character. Therefore, you should know that I AM guarding all your tomorrows, as promised.

You committed them to My keeping, didn't you?

Yours with Eternal Vigilance,
Dad

134

II Cor. 8:12 | **15**

Worried One,

I evaluate one's giving by what one has. I never judge by what one does not possess.
Remember this.

With Gratitude and Mercy,
Dad

Matt. 5:43-48 | **16**

Searching Child,

So you want to be perfect, do you? Then start showing patience with the imperfect! Lavish kindness upon the insensitive, the unattractive, the irksome.

Then you'll become perfect even as I AM.

Warning: Sometimes such perfection leads to slow death by torture. Remember your Lord.

Love,
Dad

I Thess. 5:18 | **17**

Chosen Liberator,

A myriad of options surround you.

Thanksgiving will open your eyes to see them.

Helpfully,
Father

I Cor. 4:2 **18**

Trusted Restorer,

Do *you* enjoy paying hard-earned money only to receive half-hearted service? Shoddy workmanship?

Then, before you start squawking about fair pay, make sure you're actually *doing* the job. And don't forget My extra mile policy.

Loving You Always,
Father

Eph. 4:26,27 **19**

Freedom Fighter,

I can become annoyed, true enough. But I remain mad for only a moment.

I AM shaping you to become as I AM. Aren't you glad? No doubt you've noticed that those who seethe with rage around the clock suffer burnout!

Yours Helpfully,
Father

John 14:1-6 20

Loveable Inquirer,

I appreciate your open mind. Most who pride themselves in being deep thinkers prefer to ignore Jesus. An honest investigation into His story provokes questions that explode too many popular illusions.

People want to look "cool" in contemporary circles, don't they? Problem is, ignoring Jesus is a hell of a way to stay cool...

I cry about this.

Father

Rom. 13:10-14 21

Child,

Passivity paralyzes. Paralyzation invites victimization. Have you ever heard of a "sitting duck"?

Enter into Life, child! Then Life's purpose will emerge with splendor, laughing every quibbling question into irrelevance!

Helpfully,
Dad

John 15:16 | 22

Cherished One,

I choose to need you because I love you. I do not love you because I need you. I AM hoping My kind of love will overflow from you toward others.

What joy it is to have you with Me, imparting peace in Our pressured world! People mangled by manipulation need Us.

Love,
Father

Ps. 33:16-22 | 23

Scrambling Worker,

I AM slowing you down today. This is making Our world a friendlier place — if only by a fraction.

Are you rejoicing? I AM answering your prayers for sanity. Also for a loving heart.

Faithfully Yours,
Father

I Cor. 9:22-27   **24**

Lonely Warrior,

It's hard, always having to be right, isn't it? Your friends and loved ones would enjoy you more if being right made you less abrasive and more pleasant.

No one has the nerve to pass you this message. So, as usual, I have to be the "bad guy."

Ever Devoted to Your Joy,
Father

Rom. 11:6   **25**

Diligent Disciple,

Identity determines desire, and desire gives birth to behavior. What is your identity? Do you know who you are?

You will know who you are only when you know *whose* you are!

Legalism promotes uncertainty...

Always Yours, Helpfully,
Father

Ps. 31:21-24   **26**

Anguished Child,

It wasn't your fault. The evil one took advantage of your confusion and sorrow.

I love you.

> With Everlasting Devotion,
> Father

Zech. 4:6   **27**

Trusted Restorer,

Not by might, nor by power, but by My Spirit you will conquer!

It doesn't annoy Me to remind you.

> Love,
> Dad

Luke 22:25,26; I Cor. 2:1-5   **28**

Inquiring Truth Seeker,

What is spiritual authority? It is authority that springs from experience and exhibits meekness, My loving wisdom and power. It needs none of those officious-looking trappings, typical of worldly authority.

Some of My most noble shepherds wear jeans!

Love,
Dad

James 3:13 29

Adamant Warrior,

The squeaky wheel gets the grease, true enough. But in your weary world, wheels that squeak often, despite frequent lubrication, will get ignored — or scrapped and replaced!

Persistent whiners and intimidators, beware!

Yours Honestly,
Father

Rev. 1:12-18 30

Devoted Child,

Worship is not just an act of the will. It arises as a natural response when human hearts awaken to the wonder of My Presence, My Living Reality.

Peace, tender one. I AM with you! Be still, and know I AM God.

Your Almighty Refuge,
Father

Acts 19:11-20   **31**

Concerned Conqueror,

Those captivated by the occult thirst for My power. They've scrapped sterile religion to search for it elsewhere. And rightly so!

Which is worse? The mad reign of religiosity or the magic of mesmerizers? They both appear identical to Me! Only mercy-miracles can woo wounded hearts away from such slavery.

Yours Supernaturally, Naturally,
Father

What do you see?

NOVEMBER

John 15:13 1

Cherished Child,

Searing pain exploding in every nerve cell. Agonizing thirst mingled with exhaustion. Add terror, loneliness, and the outrage of jeers and obscenities coming from His tormentors!

What do you see? Does the Crucified One reflect a God looking for reasons to reject you?

Gently,
Father

Phil. 1:6 2

Treasured Child,

I love you too much to leave you. Leaving you never occurs to My mind as an option.

Conditional love does not exist in Our Kingdom!

Yours Tenderly,
Father

Isa. 30:15,18 **3**

Searching One,

You have My wisdom within you. Shhh! Peace, little one! Become quiet, and you will discover it.

With Deepest Understanding,
Father

Pr o v.. 2 7 6 5 , **4**

Trustworthy Restorer,

Beware of stifling all opposing opinions — even those arriving with blistering bluster!

Sometimes one's opponents act as friends by providing a perspective that rescues from ruin.

Not all objections imply personal rejection.

Always Yours, Helpfully,
Dad

Matt. 20:25,26 **5**

Deliberating Disciple,

What comprises scriptural church government? One primary principle: Let the

146

greatest among you become the servant of all.

Will you help establish Heaven's government in your community?

Love,
Dad

Matt. 6:22,23 — 6

Inquiring One,

Have you noticed how hypocrites can always spot other hypocrites? Nothing delights a hypocrite more than exposing another's flaws.

Thank you for showing love, kindness and mercy.

With Deepest Gratitude,
Dad

Rom. 8:33,34 — 7

Mighty Conqueror,

Satan accused you of what?! Shame on him! Christ's blood obliterates shame for you, child.

Forever!
Dad

I Cor. 13:1-3; Gal. 5:6 **8**

Cherished One,

People who are ever looking for ways to love perform miracles. Of course, most of them would roar with laughter if anyone told them!

I don't mind...

Father

I Sam 18:11 **9**

Abused Child,

David refused to retaliate against King Saul's abuse. Yet he did dodge the spears his oppressor hurled at him!

One can love from a distance if necessary. Trust Me to lead you.

With Deepest Compassion,
Father

Rom. 11; Rom. 12:1-3 **10**

Faithful Conqueror,

Insecure personalities can't afford the luxury of meekness.

I appreciate your tender heart for those plundering the world to find their identities.

Proud of Our Partnership,
Father

Phil. 3:12 **11**

Stressed Warrior,

I just want to say how I appreciate your not giving up. I AM looking for faithfulness, not flawlessness.

Love,
Dad

Gen. 3:4,5 **12**

Inquiring Child,

The greatest sin? Buying the lie that happiness can happen apart from My Loving Presence!

Again, I forgive you.

With All My Heart,
Father

Ps. 63 **13**

Persistent Seeker,

Later on I'll address the issue you want to

talk about. Right now, I want to talk about *worship*.

Do you really believe that taking time to delight in My love will delay the help you are seeking?

Everlastingly Yours,
Father

Isa. 46:3,4 | 14

Thoughtful One,

I will not allow you to suffer abandonment in old age. Your sunset years promise a harvest of success, saturated with multiplied kindness and mercy.

Hold to this promise! It is yours.

Faithfully,
Father

John 15:5 | 15

Frenzied Freedom Fighter,

I AM not asking you to change your habits, weary child. I only ask that you bask in My love.

Sounds somehow too simple, doesn't it?

Your world underestimates the might of Omnipotent Love.

Faithfully,
Father

John 6:16-21　16

Questioning One,

Why do I usually seem to show up at the last minute? You're destined to enjoy eternal rulership with Me. For this, the one character trait you'll need most is endurance. Believe Me!

Dad

Ps. 37:3-5; Mark 9:41　17

Willing Worker,

Do what you wish, child! Forget all the stereotypes you've ever formed about "ministry."

We need more carpenters, artists, technicians and *especially* more willing workers advancing Our Kingdom. Real moms and dads are desperately needed.

Ever Delighted to Back You,
Father

II Tim. 2:13 | 18

Tired Trooper,

You may as well decide never to give up on Me. Whatever you do, I will never give up on you.

Make it easy on yourself! Everlasting Love just doesn't know how to stop loving.

Truly,
Father

Rom. 15:1-7 | 19

Restless Child,

I understand. Most church rigmarole bores Me as well. But I AM devoted, incurably devoted, to people. Would you have Me abandon them?

What if I made it a policy to abandon you when you fall short of My expectations?

Yours Patiently,
Father

John 6:28,29 20

Little One,

How can you accomplish the works of God? Rely on Jesus. Believe in Jesus. Trust in Jesus. Look to Jesus. Rest in Jesus, receiving His loving nurture.

Yours Faithfully,
Father

Luke 10:18-20 21

Searcher,

You heard Me right the first time! Go in peace. My loving wisdom saturates your spirit.

Forever Yours,
Father

I Cor. 2:9-12 22

Discouraged Child,

Yes, you live in a harsh world, little one. It's a world that exhibits little patience with inexperience, lack of knowledge or ineptitude.

Quickly pray in the spirit! Wisdom that laughs at earthly logic awaits you. It's time We boggled a few minds!

Love,
Dad

Prov. 6:16-19 **23**

Inquiring Child,

What provokes My rage? Proud hypocrisy! Looking for loopholes to get around having to care about people. Betraying confidences. Double-dealing that repays trust with treachery! Slander. Self-promotion that achieves its goals by inflaming friend against friend.

Yours Faithfully,
Father

Prov. 14:12; Rom. 8:13-15 **24**

Truth Seeker,

Pursue balance and you'll find only corrupting compromise. Follow Me, and I will bring you into balance.

And just for the record: I AM *not* religious!

Love,
Dad

Dan. 10:12,13 — 25

Bewildered One,

Sometimes your prayers provoke resistance from hell. Our enemy hopes you will accuse Me of responding to your requests with treachery.

Do you remember the old tactic called "divide and conquer"?

Yours Entreatingly,
Father

Rom. 7; Rom. 8 — 26

Distraught Child,

I know your heart. I do understand you. I realize that you yearn above all else to walk in My will — except for those times when you don't!

I sent Jesus to heal this schizophrenia common among mortals. Resume walking with Me, and rest in My love.

Dad

James 3:13

27

Faithful One,

Some people prefer being "right" to being healed. I have plopped you in the midst of such madness to function as a stabilizer — not to speak or expound, but to function.

Just rely on My Unction, and function!

Proudly Yours,
Dad

I Cor. 1:3

28

Remorseful Child,

What are you talking about? Don't bother refreshing My memory of any sin already forgiven.

With Love Everlasting,
Dad

Prov. 3:5,6

29

Truth Seeker,

Trust Me with all your heart. Refuse to rely on your own reasoning. In all your comings and goings enjoy fellowship with Me, and I will direct your steps. Sounds somehow "biblical," doesn't it?

With Joy,
Father

Rom. 5:8 **30**

Diligent Disciple,

Thank you for loving people more than you cherish perfection. Such love gave birth to the New Testament, didn't it? My Son's cross reveals the cost of such love.

Draw near, weary one. Receive My refreshment.

Yours Devotedly,
Father

*Like eagles,
they soar above
the world's chaos.*

DECEMBER

Child,

What happens to those who hope in Me? To those who wait in My Presence? They grow strong both in body and spirit. Like eagles, they soar above the world's chaos. They run without weariness. They can walk, and walk, and walk — and yet never succumb to despair.

Just a reminder...

Dad

Inquiring Child,

Frankly, you're not asking for too much, but for too little. I've hesitated to respond to your requests for this reason.

Quiet your heart in My Presence, and re-assess your requests! I long to lavish abundance upon you.

Your All Sufficient Father

II Tim. 4:3-5 | 3

Bored Browser,

People who are serious about walking in My will also hold My opinions in highest regard.

How are you coming along with the last revelation I gave you?

Just asking...

Father

I John 4:16 | 4

Frustrated Seeker,

You're absolutely right. I do as I please, and nothing can stop Me!

Isn't it wonderful to know that My loving heart governs all of My actions?

Thank you for trusting!

Father

Phil. 3:1 | 5

Weary One,

What if repeating Myself again and again made *Me* irritable and nervous?

Think about it.

HA!
Dad

Isa. 54:17   **6**

Fatigued Freedom Fighter,

You are Mine. No weapon — again, I say — no weapon forged against you will prosper! Cease fretting, child. You yearn for My will, so you walk in My will. My glory surrounds and shields you.

Love,
Father

II Cor. 2:14   **7**

Child,

I know your anguish, and I promise! No evil will triumph over you. I will see to it.

With Deepest Compassion,
Father

Ps. 103:10-14   **8**

Weary-Hearted One,

While you've been groveling and trying

to atone for your sins, I've been maneuvering you into position to receive this message: STOP! Please, tender one.

Let's resume Our adventure.

Love,
Dad

Matt. 5:37 **9**

Pressured One,

No! A hard word to say, isn't it? You must try it sometime. I will help you. The peace that results will amaze you.

Dad

Jer. 1:5-8 **10**

Trembling Restorer,

Don't worry about words. You are My message! Each day I AM shaping you to become what is needed for your every encounter.

Just to confirm!

Love,
Dad

Phil. 4:6, 7   **11**

Child,

Knowing why will never satisfy you like experiencing My power. Taste and see. Enter into praise, and enjoy!

I think you're wonderful.

Love,
Dad

Eph. 1:3-8   **12**

Nervous Adventurer,

Just to confirm your suspicions... I AM out to get you! When I catch you, you'll wonder why you ever tried to avoid Me.

Father

Ps. 46:10   **13**

Tired Trooper,

Learn to resist rushing, last-minute scrambling, stampeding! Steady plodding saves a soul from many a snare.

View sudden rearrangements as rescues.

Faithfully,
Father

I Cor. 6:18-20

14

Restless One,

What do you do when lust nibbles at your emotions? Flee! Run for your life! I mean this.

Your Invincible Refuge,
Father

Ps. 131

15

Child,

It doesn't matter, it doesn't matter, it just doesn't matter!

Peace, little one. All that matters is Us.

Truthfully, Compassionately,
Father

Matt. 26:59-63

16

Strong Conqueror,

This time refuse to retreat into self pity. You can love opinionated people while ignoring their noise. Shouldn't I know?

Smiling with You,
Father

Gal. 5:25 **17**

Faithful Child,

Keep it simple! It is possible. Just follow Me.

Father

Acts 8:18-24 **18**

Beloved Liberator,

I understand your feelings. But it's wrong to rebuke the world for commercializing Christmas. Unfortunately, some of My clever children started this trend!

Trying to buy love and respect with tinseled packages, little one, trivializes the glad tidings of Jesus.

I know you would never want to do that.

Devoted to You Always,

Father

Ps. 33:1-5 **19**

Cherished One,

Thank you for keeping Me informed. When can We just enjoy One Another?

I treasure your friendship.

Father

Ps. 32:1,2 **20**

Grieving Child,

Apology accepted. Now forgive yourself.

Tenderly,
Father

Rev. 12:10,11 **21**

Loveable Truth Seeker,

Don't listen to lies. Any "spiritual revelation" eroding trust in My grace is a lie.

You know the Truth. Enjoy your freedom!

Forever Yours,
Father

Phil. 3:12-15 **22**

Strong Conqueror,

The more you learn to dwell with Me in the present, the more foreign the memories of old pursuits will appear when they crop up on occasion.

This is why I keep "harping" about the perils of self-scrutiny unsanctioned by Me.

Love,
Dad

Isa. 29:13,14; Matt. 7:21 **23**

Child,

I love you too much to let you substitute ritual for relationship.

Dad

Luke 2:13,14 **24**

Zealous Warrior,

When Heaven's angels heralded My Son's arrival in your world, did they proclaim wrath and destruction on earth and misery for all men? Or did they announce peace on earth and good will to all men?

Don't forget! Gospel means *good news*!

Love,
Dad

DECEMBER

I Pet. 1:18,19

25

Cherished Child,

No one can buy you! You are far too costly. Your value equals that of your Lord. And His value defies all computation!

Return all gifts that arrive with strings attached, child. Quickly! Post haste! Yesterday!!

Always Your Ally,
Dad

Matt. 20:1-16

26

Little One,

What? Not one of My children has ever paid his or her dues! Doesn't such thinking betray forgetfulness of Calvary?

Yours Faithfully,
Dad

Ps. 31:23,24

27

Tender-Hearted One,

Those giving you a hard time are mad at Me, not you. Respond with tact. Be patient. I will soon render you unavailable. Relieved?

Your Rock of Refuge Always,

Dad

Luke 14:7-11 28

Child,

Cease demanding respect, and you will receive it. Seek honor, and you'll become the target of jokes and contempt.

Just be you. Do you mind? I like you. Sorry if repeating Myself disturbs your sense of good style.

Love,

Dad

Ps. 31:17 29

Tender One,

I have seen your tears and heard your cries. I've walked with you through sorrows which only you and I have known.

And satan tells you I plan humiliation and grief for you? Don't believe a word of it!

Tenderly,

Father

Matt. 6:1-4 — 30

Delightful Child,

But I love bragging about you in front of your fellow workers and friends!

How can you get Me to stop? Simple enough. Just start singing your own praises, and I'll clam up immediately.

Yours Cheerfully,
Dad

Luke 15:14-17 — 31

Exploding Explorer,

When rage erupts for having endured unreality's mad tyranny, one has reached the road to recovery.

Am I glad you are mad — at long last! Now We can get on with your life.

With Exuberant Delight!
Father

POSTSCRIPT

Good news! You can enjoy intimacy and real communication with our Creator, Father God. How?

Sincerely choose to trust and declare:

(1) that Jesus Christ is His only begotten Son and Lord of creation.

(2) that He died and rose again by God's power to adopt you into His royal family (Rom. 10:9,10).

Perhaps repeating this prayer will help you:

Heavenly Father,

Thank you for sending Jesus Christ, Your only Son. I believe the good news that He died to deliver me from the hell of existing apart from your Presence. Thank you for raising Him to life again. I acknowledge Jesus as my Lord, and I now welcome knowing You as My gracious Father on

_____ _____ _____ ,
(Month)   (Day)   (Year)

Amen, and so be it!

_____ (Signed)

171

Made in United States
Orlando, FL
04 May 2023

32785062R00102